BEATS OF THE HEART

By

Girlie E. Catanus

Edited by Marie Ezekiel
Arranged by Tess Ritumalta

ISBN:
oftbound/Paperback-978-621-470-259-6
Hardbound-978-621-470-260-2
MOBI/KINDLE-978-621-470-261-9

Published by:
Poetry Planet Book Publishing House
Rosario, Pozorrubio, Pangasinan, Philippines
Contact No.: 09554960044
Email: maritesritumalta@gmail.com

DEDICATION

To my dear Nanay Helen and Tatay Oming for your unwavering love, encouragement, and support. You are always my inspiration and the very first reason why I always strive to improve and prove to myself that I can always do better. I am so honored and proud to have you both. Wherever you are, I know you are happy seeing us achieving our dreams in life. I love you so much.

ACKNOWLEDGEMENT

The author is extending her warm gratitude for the very inspiring support of special people in their assistance in pursuing to publish of a book, hereby;

Mrs. Isidra A. Cagatan, her mentor for sharing her insights and expertise in writing a poem;

Zach Zyan and Zai Zedric, her sons who have been a source of source of courage and inspiration to pursue this underlying to its completion;

Zacarias, her husband, for patient, understanding, and unconditional love which generated her courage and inspiration;

Her sisters for their shared knowledge and care for her children during the entire process;

Above all, the **God Almighty** whose blessings made the researcher strong and determined to attain her goal.

TABLE OF CONTENTS

Copyright 2

Dedication 3

True Friends 8

Lord, Keep Us Safe 10

We Love Each Other Everyday 11

Thank You Lord...............................12

Be Thankful 13

Heart Oh! Heart..............................14

Enchanted River.............................15

Auspicious 16

Beautiful Girl 17

Smile 18

Sunday 19

God Is Good All The Time 20

Thank You 2019 21

Collide..23

Mistletoe Kiss 25

Congrats And Best Wishes 26

It's Been A While............................27

Unheard Plea..................................28

Loving You Forever.........................29

Humble Your Heart.....................31

United Nations 33

Teachers 34

Face Maskless Time.....................36

Radio 37

Poetry Is Painting That Speaks 38

Water Is Life 39

Butterfly 40

Oblivion 41

Be Hopeful 42

The Romancer 43

Essence Of Life.....................44

Poetic Plead.....................45

The Brave.....................46

Morning Sky 47

World Exploration 48

I Believe.....................51

Midnight Dew 52

On The Wings Of Love.....................54

Teenage Love 55

Promised Love 56

Mixed Feelings.....................57

I Believe.....................58

Amazing Love...59

More Than Just A Treasure..........................60

Year 2020..61

What If? 63

God Be With You 64

Nature's Way 66

Rewrite The Star 67

About The Author 69

TRUE FRIENDS

They don't go away from you thru thick and thin
They are your supporters whatever
But if you feel they won't they aren't true friends
Go away from them, they are just Tupperware.

True friends tell you frankly the good and bad points
If they can't, think over who they are
They are your buddies though in silence and vulgar
They fight for your right and they don't scare you.

True friends are not selfish they are willing to share
They are always willing to give than to receive
They don't envy your success but believe
They are happy and gay if something is achieved.

True friends don't talk behind your back
But correct your misdemeanors if you have
Guide you on a straight path
Cheer you when you feel sad.

If your treated true friends don't belong on the list
It's up for you to make your own revised
This is mine for this is what I did
To all my friends if I failed to do these

I am not your true friend.
I just belong to some acquaintances
A meanwhile friend but not the truest friend
That you can lean.

LORD, KEEP US SAFE

Keep us safe all the time
We are pleading with your merciful eyes
To look upon us every now and then
We trust you forever all the time.

Lord God, our faith in you is our life
In your hand, we commend our soul and mind
Please keep us in a safe place of love
Where life is purposeful and more defined.

Take away the threats that surround us
Rest assured our living is safe and prosperous
All of us the children and the older ones
Keep us safe against any harm natural or manmade.

No one can give us the assurance but you
Not even the richest and powerful here in the U
You alone our God has the prerogative to do so
We are now strengthening our faith in you.

We believe you, we adore you.
We only trust to our God Its You
The most trusting worth believing yes You
From yesterday, today and tomorrow. Amen

WE LOVE EACH OTHER EVERYDAY

Your love is the sweetest thing that happens to me
My love for you is the bravest thing I've ever shown
away
We love each other as we always be
The love that we nurtured day by day
The *kilig* moments every time I look at you
It gets more from time to time as the days go
The experience of being a newlywed continues
I love you so much my daddy dearie
And I can feel the same the love you bestow on me
Nothing has been subtracted instead more added
daddy
I love you more each day daddy my sweetie.
For us, every day is a Valentine's day
I want to cling with you my dearie daddy
Our two boys are the witness to the sweet love we do
each day
They are our cheerers and the critics as they want to
be.
With God's graces and blessings, this will last
Until we get very old at that
Even you and I will wear with white hair flash
We together forever walk hand in hand.
God bless us all the time every second, minute, hour
and day long
We are strengthened with faith and trust in God alone
He always gives us the love so strong
This is the proof of love as we go along

THANK YOU, LORD

We have so many things to thank in God
Our lives and the provisions we had
The people around us through thick and thin
They are the ones we can call loyal friends.

Thank you, Lord, for every piece of bread we eat
For every rice grain, we cook always
For the pieces of fish
For the meat of a pig.

All these things around us are from God
We cannot possess this without God
The great provider that loved us
And perpetually help us guide us.

Lord thank you also for the down moments
It helped us a lot to learn
The lessons in life we bear
You are really balanced and great.

You are our great master
We can lean on you at all times
You are the best ever
The only God we praise forever.

BE THANKFUL

Every breath we take is free
We could not get it anyway
Be thankful God provides it for you and me
We have no right to blame him all the way.

All our possessions are from God
We are just the trusted tenants
Would you not be thankful for all of that?
My God how ungrateful we are to God.

Be thankful for a piece of bread you eat
For a piece of fish, a cup of rice, and health you keep
All of these are worth thanking for so deep
My God how I am really thankful for that.

A very simple gift we receive makes us happy
How much more the life God gave to me
Oh my God! So sorry oh sorry
For not giving praise for all the kindness you gave to
me

But now I do really oh really.
I want to thank you Lord every day
Every second, minute, and hour of the day
Hail! My God my only God I love thee!

HEART OH! HEART

The pumping station of our body
The most delicate part of the Circulatory
You are so essential oh! Hearty
You must be healthy all the way.

I am pleading to the God Almighty
Please heal the heart of my *kumare*
Clean her vein and artery
So that the blood will flow freely.

To all the people in this world
I am just warning you all
To your heart please be careful
Because heart ailment is a traitor.

If you feel something wrong
Mind it and find a cure
Do not wait for a doctor
To have you spend more.

The heart is a sign of love
Its normal sound is lub-dub
It's everybody's goal to have
A healthy loving heart

ENCHANTED RIVER

A lone place before
Told by our ancestors
A river so mysterious
So wondrous how it causes.

A river that enchants you
For it has a beautiful view
Water is so inviting to go thru
Only nature haters can't appreciate you.

So unexplainable nature
What in this world
Head of the river that no core
Fishes swimming more and more.

Water so cold like the fountain of ice
Its clearness that captivates our eyes
A lot of visitors abide
The law of beauty might.

Enchanted when we were young
We come and go beyond
We didn't expect your fame upon
So inviting the nation to abound.

Enchanted River is our very own
Thank God for this nice creature
It paves the residents more favors
Opportunity to extend hard work.

AUSPICIOUS

Failures come and go
Besides, never let it do
Don't make any remnants at you
For it can suppress and undo

Positivity of someone exists
Look always at the bright side
Of life and the thing that keeps
That is standing up beyond the test.

Keep strong as you ever have
Be the enlightenment to the mob
Uphold the right and correct
Live the positive notion that is set.

Read the epistles of the apostles
They unearth the things untold
Give us some gauge of good emotion
This is your edge to no passion.

Strive and struggle to reach
The unreachable dates
The days and years in the universe
They are but just to craze.

You are born free
God provides many
Favors and possibility
So be auspicious as you can be.

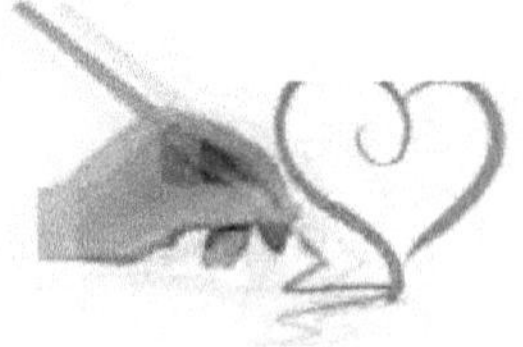

BEAUTIFUL GIRL

Wherever you are
You have a pure heart
That you treasure much
One of a kind at such

Anna baby besides being busy
Still, you manage your beauty
Your slim and sexy body
Only blinds cannot see

OH! Young and beautiful Anna
Be selective but don't wanna
Be choosy that you gonna
Forget the days of old *harana*...

If you don't mind baby
Let me interfere oh! Dearie
When will you get marry
OH! Darling sweet lady.

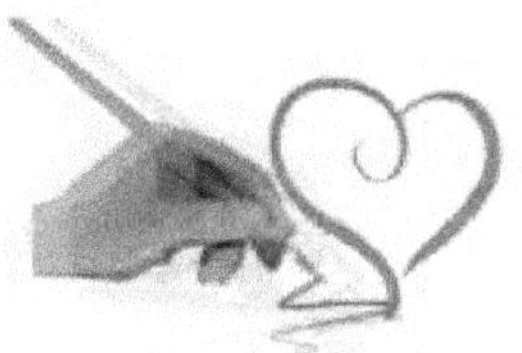

SMILE

It shows a positive feeling
Happiness in the inner being
Invites a friendly intermingling
A smile can ease a deeper thinking

Not everyone who smiles is truly happy
Sometimes it's just a facade of feeling lonely
But a smile touches a bounded heart for free
Let the smile govern and be gay.

Smile my darling friend
Everything in life is so kind
God will grant us a peace of mind
Real happiness is in smilin'.

A smile is a bond of happy souls
Can create a true loving goals
Surpasses many life downfalls
Open your mouth and smile at all.

Let us smile wherever we are
Don't be selfish to give and share
A smiling one can never depart
A happy life has a pure heart.

SUNDAY

A great day everybody awaits
A day to worship and celebrate
Though every day is God's faith
But Sunday should not be missed

Sunday Oh! Sunday is a holiday!
Its essence brings inner meaning to many
We love you Sunday, today, and every day
Today is a sunny Sunday

For children, Sunday is for bonding
Daddy, mommy, and children
Go somewhere to eat others go swimming
A happy Sunday a time of regaining

Sunday is for family
Daddy, mommy, and baby day
It's very nice to say
Hello! We love each other every day.

GOD IS GOOD ALL THE TIME

Many trials may come our way
But we wonder why we're still okay
God made the best remedy
With our strong faith in God, we stay

Every day is more wonderful
How we live a life so joyful
God is miraculous and helpful
He provides us with life that's meaningful

Sometimes other people feel frustrated
To live a life full of threats
They are just a test of faith
The truth is God awaits

God is good all the time
He never leaves us unmind
Trust in him for all your problems
You just awake everything is fine.

THANK YOU 2019

I have so much to thank for
By the graces of our Lord
Petit things that blest me more
Without God would stay impossible.

Here I am standing with good health
My mother and the whole family are equipped
With so much love and faith
I am now a certified poetess.

As a teacher, I had extended a lot of help
To some pupils who need a coaching tip
In my own little ways, I have shared my adept
To the least who wanted to be straight.

In 2019 God heard my longingness
To serve more like one of the teachers' coaches
I have gone through a lot of struggles but God enriched
My mind and heart to extend his graces.

I am not a hypocrite to say I don't need wealth
Which everybody craves to possess it
I know God would provide in his bet
Grateful me oh! 2019 for all of these so great.

Lord God, thank 2019 in all your ways
Be pursued through the years of next
Continue OH! Lord the things you blest
For me and my family as we wished.

Thank you 2019 and the years to come
Thank you, Lord, God Jesus Christ for what you have
done
In our lives, now and forever we worship you alone
You are the light and lifeguard that to us watching up
and down.

COLLIDE

In life, there is what we call a blessing in disguise
An encounter suddenly happened with a prize
That makes sense in life's journey as a surprise
You are the one that gives me a wholesome life.

I need not to stay without you and me abide
You are my life that God sent me as we collide
I must not astray in this world I don't hide
But thankful enough to have you before I die.

I must obey the dictate of my heartbeat
I don't accept it, in the way, there is defeat
This is my destiny, to have you on my fate
It's you my dearest who keeps my faith.

You alone give me a colorful fight
You are the one I dream of at night
To be with you is my ultimate light
Shining in front, to show me a glittering sight.

Our collide was an honest fulfilling incident
That brought us to a faithful coincidence
You are my wish no more accident
The collision happened for a milestone increment.

I don't need what yesterday and tomorrow would
bring
I only have you in my life would be rewarding
You are the only one that I dream of thing
The best one that I keep on my feeling.

What I want is you alone please don't leave
I will strive hard to be with you while am alive
You and me as one forever we live
Promise my darling our collide leads us to be united.

MISTLETOE KISS

Your sweet lips' kiss, mark on my face
This Christmas I send you a card
Find my socks and a bell rings to race
Mistletoe, your green leaves at a vase

Uttering words tight hugs reward
Your sweet lips kiss, mark on my face
I found your tender love caress
Swinging high upward and downward
Find my socks and a bell rings to race

Hang on this Christmas from EastWest
Gleeful carols of shepherds based
Your sweet lips' kiss, mark on my face
Hi! hey hoo, come on let's go craze

So that everybody will be amazed
Find my socks and a bell rings to race
Am just a human who must seize
In a mistletoe kiss, I daze
Your sweet lips kiss, mark on my face
Find my socks and a bell rings to race.

CONGRATS AND BEST WISHES

Your love flies flawlessly in the sense
Here you are saying your vows in our presence
You both promise to live with God's magnificence
For today you are united as one great imminence.

We witness today your union
You are in love in unison
Forever you will live with aspirations
You are building a family with full motivation.

Joan loves Kanette Ace thru thick and thin
Together you will share each other then
Offer your best of everything
For being a husband and wife everlasting.

Whatever rains and rainbows hinder you
Stay loving intimately which shows
The epitome of God's creature
As one, you bear the family's nature.

Thriving your family in all manners
As one, you never give up nor surrender
Instead, help each other
Always nurture your love forever.

IT'S BEEN A WHILE

Looking back for where did we belong
Singing a melancholic song
Loud and clear but we did go wrong
Suddenly, solitude reminds me of a monk.

It's been a while of not doing the way we used to be
The sudden burst of emotions downloaded abruptly
Thinking so much of brokenness of doubted scrutiny
Picking up the scattered pieces of many.

The mastery of the non-sense application
Making the most stories of clarification
Longing to the numerous pondered actions
That for a moment awaits your interaction.

Oh! it's been a while of no motion
Static in a nook of no sensation
Bothered and annoyed by some notions
Crafted along with overwhelming satiation.

A vivid imagination lost its command
Transformed into a blurred instant
Dominating the predicament so hesitant
To establish a meaningful life plan.

UNHEARD PLEA

Tired of sending an utmost emotion
No one hears, no one cares even negation
Sad to know the real score of inhibition
It's just to ignore and still hang on.

The worst setting for one's companion
What should we do if not counted on
Just stay calm and look upon
God will answer the plea on his own.

No feeling of empathy
There's no way to stay
Deadmatic strategic dismay
Above all rude to someone or many.

Please listen to this to whisper hope
Attain the little feelings of nope
Open your heart with a scoop
Measure the unmeasured scope.

LOVING YOU FOREVER

From the very start of our growing love
I thanked our dear Father God above
For having you in my life through thick and thin
Standing by my side from now and then.

You are the answer to my wholehearted prayer
That continually nourishes and fails never
You sustain me as my lifelong partner
You were steadfast in all trials that hinder you.

You give me happiness that pursues through the years
You lift me up when I feel bad you transfo0rm it
better
You are the only one I long to be forever
No one could fill me up except you my dear.

When we face the altar for our long time vow
I said to God, this is the man who taught me how
To be with me in all life's journey as I bow
For respect and doses of love as thou.

For sixteen years of loving you
I can prove to the world that love must go through
I need no one to be with but only you
You make me complete with our kids too.

Everyday to be with you is something fulfilling
We surpassed the challenges of life worth
remembering
Together we build a happy home laughing
We promised each other to live and love satisfying.

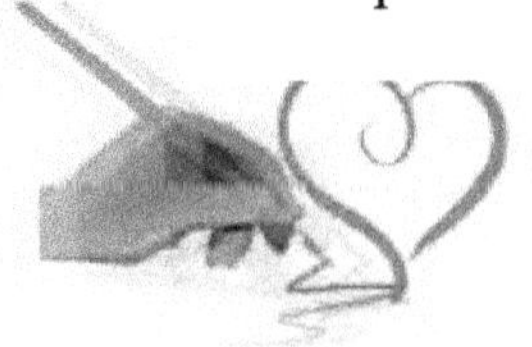

When you look at me, I can feel your sparkling eye
Your inviting lips that add your sweet smile
Embracing me through the unending night
Of love and passion like the first time.

My darling my sweet hubby dear
Our children are the proof of love so tender
The renewal of vows let's cheer
For more dozen of sweetness together.

I won't get tired to be expressive of what I feel
I will always stand as your loving wife with a thrill
Thriving our family as to strongly built
You and I our kids will still.

HUMBLE YOUR HEART

Look fairly to the Earth
The creation of God deserves
The most isotactic treat
Live with utmost love no dirt.

Whoever you are in a high ranking position
In God's eyes, we are all equally mentioned
No one is above the other in God's attention
No tags in Him no favorites in his intention.

Faithfully we are one in His eyes
We have no right to make ourselves high
For in God, we are all creations we all tend to die
In His time we would go back to ashes with no teary
eyes.

We all have, ourselves' restrictions
Our own mandates with demanding provocation
Did you try to consult God in your decision?
Did he give you a go signal as you go on?

God is fair and humble
Never He allows anyone to stumble
He wants us to be helpful
Loving to fellows, considerate and understandable.

Unlock your selfish heart
Try it deeply to depart
Earthly matters are just to attract
But God's love is constantly on track.

Humble your heart great hypocrite
Lower your belt
Down your ego to deep Earth
Look around the hurting feelings you shared
Renew your ways, and align them to God's
faithfulness.

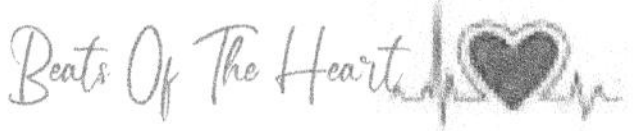

UNITED NATIONS

Different skin colors
Varied also in religions
In riches and regions
From east to west dimensions.

Some are white and rich
Others are just moderate
From the nearest to farthest
But united we are as God's image

I am from the Philippines
You might be from the US
Or from other states
We are one now as we celebrate.

One mind, one aims to uphold
As an objective to unite as a whole
Reaching from the south pole to the north pole
We are the United Nations' symbol.

We are the children to represent the future
We need this to nurture
United as one as we all face the great picture
Of a triumphant and successful nature.

TEACHERS

Wherever we are, in this world
With the same objectives to uphold
Bearing the tasks to enfold
Until the time of getting old.

Teachers are the unsung heroes
Some were victims of the pandemic now they loss
While living we must continue to engross
The essence of our lives to outburst.

On this very day, let's have a break
Inhale and inhale the air we take
Capturing the moment we ought to seek
Releasing the emotions we long to make.

We have tried to cross the rivers to reach out
The learners we cannot touch about
Dialing the phone we felt calloused
Stay ringing but no one to talk to.

Our heartbeats are palpitating
We have a mind of worrying
We even have a nightmare while sleeping
What might we leave one child behind.

Every time our notification pops up
There must be a hurried report to pass
That we should attain immediately to cope
Stressful yet fulfilling that we had done those.

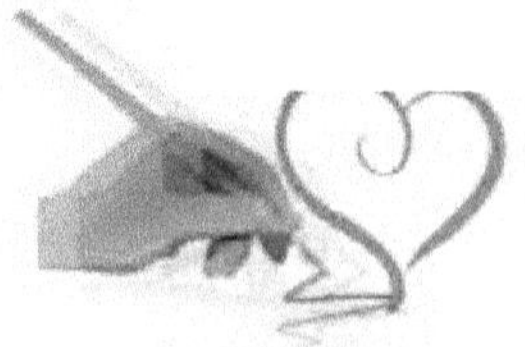

Teachers of today why should we do this?
Making initiatives and some remedies
To instill learning in various modalities
Pandemic please go away for we prefer face to face.

Let's be steadfast and stay firm to adhere
For the best of children's welfare
No single task we miss to prepare
For the love to our learners.

FACE MASKLESS TIME

A time when I could go freely
With my own energetically
Anywhere, everywhere whole day
Fearless, no hazard around me.

I can show my smile to the world
I can reach the places all aboard
I can hug my comrades closely on the road
Have a tete-a-tete nearly of some words.

When can I experience this face maskless time?
When now, we have an Enhance Community
Quarantine?
Stay at home Delta Variant is scaring thine
For one and a half years it's hindering our family to
out dine.

Face maskless time connotes our liberty
Of being imprisoned in this pandemic vanity
The freedom to explore, breathing fresh air naturally
Walking on the paddocks of campuses vigorously.

RADIO

You bring us great delight
Listening to the songs upright
The lyrics we long outright
The love of our sight.

Throwback remembering
Provincial lives were lingering
The lifestyle we are longing
Now we are renewing.

Oh my radio,
Glad to be with you
Whispering moments anew
Songs of life give clues.

Music is life ooohhh...
This is a feeling so true
Reminding long ago
Having our new radio.

POETRY IS PAINTING THAT SPEAKS

They are lines that penetrate to our inner being
They truly speak straight to our shoulders no lying
Words from the heart of a poetess writing
That to other people reminds us to keep reading.

Immeasurable thoughts maniefest the depth of feeling
The sanctuary of ideas is intertwining
From one mind to another interlinking
Somehow intangible notions are reminded.

Go! walk in the wilderness of my pen
Search the deepest feelings from within
Unearth the principles long ago were hidden
Move on and face the reality that soon will happen.

Let's ink the woven words in your mind
Express the meaning of life behind
Try to linger the occurrence of something undefined
Unfold the stressful events of life to be refined.

WATER IS LIFE

Of a sudden no more water
I almost fell my tear
For water is life no matter
We need it now and forever.

Rain is always falling down
Immediately on the ground
We need potable water around
Please let it flow abound.

A clean and drinking water
That quenches our thirst
Cleanses our body and dirt
Please come in some minutes.

We can survive with no food for a week
But water is a different story to take
It has oxygen that removes some aches
We are not sure how long it partakes.

Cooking is impossible with no water
How can we satisfy our hunger?
Taking a bath is no longer
A mixture of smells appears.

Anyway, this is a short sacrifice
Than that of our Lord Jesus Christ
We must be patient and cease our lies
Repent and spread the love as a prize.

BUTTERFLY

The life of a butterfly has stages
Starting to turn to many pages
As a miniature relating messages
Driving at different anchorages.

It has a delightful life on the flowers bloom
That gives a meaningful glance at the gloom
Sipping the nectar of a flower at zoom
Inviting the beautiful bride and groom.

Crafted mind flies at high inside and out
Trusting its wings with no doubt
Reflected memories so stout
Playing games all about.

This is a continuous process of life grows
Towards the straight columns and rows
Mind-sets arranging the meaningful blows
Seeking for utmost happiness that glows.

OBLIVION

You know me well first and foremost
But it seemed that I was lost
In your friends' list of utmost
You treated me like a ghost.

Hurray! for it satisfied your soul
Doubted me, it's my downfall
Putting me to bin of trashes at all
Not me, my friend and walk away to the hall.

I was horrified by your treatment
Belittled like a kid at the moment
Throwing me away, a punishment
Of a forgotten comrade at a sudden.

Never do I need to revenge
Nothing in my heart a change
To create a negative challenge
For me, you are always within.

Beseeching to Lord God to bring back
All your normal memories unpacked
Come again let us talk intact
To glorify his name at the dock.

BE HOPEFUL

I'll be happy once I've done this certain thing
That can help our world now too much worrying
Of the health issues that keep us hindering
I am here faithful to God and always praying.

Much needed now is our unity to find ways
We have some vaccines let's not waste
The time is here for each one to cooperate
Ponder ourselves by having us participate.

We have to follow carefully some protocols
Needed to stay healthy amidst the blindfold
Of horrified individuals in this weary world
Do something that can contribute to the call.

Life is our precious ownership to uphold
Let's love it and nurture each one untold
Be the model of life's best we all mold
Standstill fortified by God and prayers unfold.

THE ROMANCER

Thinking the same negative thought
That buried myself as I caught
The brainstorming that brought
Some valid reasons were never sought.

An empty space of a groovy romancer
Set aside the gloomy morn appear
Clinging to her masked provider
Zooming the blurred notions seeker.

Replicated it for a numerous moments
Hiding the truest predicaments
Subsided in a resurrected vehement
Passing over to the farthest placement.

The sighs and musings of some habitants
Never heard for they were all reluctant
Realizing that someday might be relevant
To the present scenario of no vacant.

The tiny light has shown a new hope
Announced today by our dear Pope
We can allow them to cope
With the latest aim and scope.

ESSENCE OF LIFE

As I walk on the paddocks of nothing
I realized the essence of my life
I cried out loud for my triumphant existence
Savored with my atmospheric eloquence.

As I pursued my journey here I am alone
No one to talk to, no one to hold on
In this high humidity temperature
I manage to stand with my weak bones

I face gradually the blank hue of tomorrow.
Enumerate my misdemeanors my dear
Where did I go wrong that kept me slumber
Hiding the truth I long to reveal

Mesmerizing in front of me a bit.
Tell me would I be mistaken?
If I lied to save the lives of many
Or did I manipulate the non-sense
I do believe it would be for everybody's betterment.

POETIC PLEAD

You are an extraordinary field
Where everyone loves to explore with
Weaving words, touching hearts indeed
A literary connection which we uplifted.

Poetry warms the cold zones of oblivion
Energizes the nerves of transformation
Interlinks the world of various nations
Revives the thoughts into heartfelt transpiration.

You give me a burning inspiration
Whenever I pen my heart that jerks for admiration
Sustaining my enthusiastic mind to live with
courageous domestication
Gives me a lot of a vivid vision.

In these trying times when an invisible opponents
attack
You are our weapon that keeps us intact
You bind us together to ease our fearful track
That holds us on beneath the losing impact.

Oh, poetry! you are my handful therapy
Whenever I feel bad and lonely
I just ink my emotion and I get well immediately
For a dose of words, I write that heals me
automatically.

THE BRAVE

Ready to face the utmost reality
Whether in struggles or vanity
Is showing somehow a bravery
That paddles us to a certain tranquillity.

Courageous and fearless battle against poverty
Fighting nonetheless for the whole of humanity
Fully geared with passion and love for the family
Then you are the heroine of your own activity.

Unleash the emotion-driven goal
Partake the predicament as a tool
Looking forward with no hidden soul
Not even a piece but a whole.

Bravery is not merely fighting to diminish
It is either to accept or participate to replenish
The emptiness of emotions of anguish
You are brave enough to suffice the miss.

MORNING SKY

Another hope has risen for humanity
A shining morn that lightened is universally
Embracing a new touch of life this early
Bringing a bursting love satisfactorily.

To dream is to look forward to a better tomorrow
Forgetting all we had experienced in sorrow
To go forward mild and mellow
Facing the new light and say hello.

Throwing back the old heavy luggage
Sunken memoirs deeply bridge
The non-sense acrobatic damages
The stumbling block for all ages.

Pack up now, let's walk hand in hand
Let's make a new life bond
Take all the gladiolus pieces of fun
Put to oblivion the negative runs.

Across the dimmer part of yesterday
Here we are standing firmly
Living life naturally
With us is a wide smile joyously.

WORLD EXPLORATION

I was sitting under the tree
Besides the wavy sea
Thinking of a long journey
Incapable, I have no penny.

My tired eyes were sleepy
Reminiscing a sweet memory
Escaping the reality
To no one sensibility.

The white sand dashing on my skin
Sunlight soothed to my worried brain
The seawater played within my spine
I was nearly blown by the wind.

In the jungle, the lions roared
The huge trees heightening poured
The vines bowed unto my cord
The birds sang in their accord.

The city was with its nuisance
The loud music in its annoyance
Avenues around in their extravagance
I was awakened with my wanderlust.

THE RIGHT TO WRITE

Let my bleeding pen flow
Pursue to wind up blow
Inking the words of mellow
Soothing to my bones below.

No one could stop me from writing
My ultimate chance to express my feeling
Energizes my mind, the food of my thinking
That my thirsty soul keeps longing.

My only weapon to withstand
When I feel low nothing beyond
The blank space invites my hand
To start weaving thoughts in an instance.

This is my life the truth in my imagination
To fulfill my dreams not a hallucination
A mere fact playing as my remediation
Enhancing my expertise with or without collaboration.

Amidst the misty night of darkness
Where everyone feels emptiness
Scribbling is my only happiness
That sustains my selflessness.

I must live the way I want to
As I sleep on my pillow
Realizing the essence of tomorrow
That somehow I am getting through.

The chaotic predicament of this world
Torturing our senses to get bored
Mindfulness is being restored
Lifeful grandeur style at hoard.

Until the end of time, I will write
Using my most loved right
My poetry is my light
That reflects my insights

I BELIEVE

I believe I can do it all
The heightening triumphant soul
I can fly beneath my shining tool
Bringing up the high-spirited rule

How difficult the task is
I can succeed as I practice
My strong determination sees
That I am able to do this.

Nothing is impossible my dear friend
If we are empowered to apprehend
That I strongly believe I can attain
Beholding all that pertains.

I can reach my goal as I go on
Believing firmly in my own
For the one, up above his throne
Guiding me as I perform.

Wherever I may be brought
Of my tomorrow's moving foot
I believe I can fulfill my thought
Yes, I do for my belief is for the truth.

MIDNIGHT DEW

Wintertime in a tropical place
Like our country the Philippines
Somehow I dream to feel like this
Midnight dew blows me, please.

In the polar places, they have snow
They are more or less feeling so cold
Their feathery jackets keep them warm but low
The rock of ice surrounds them so.

Midnight dew what can I do?
To make you feel that I am true
How can I convince you?
I am just mediocre in this midtown glow.

In every cooling nook, you stay
I am conveying a message you say
But the cold penetrates my whole body
Trying to stop my breath but I disagree.

The moist and hydrogenic power of you
Soothes my nerves and taps me too
So cold, so demanding to capture my whole life
through
So amazing that keeps me live all it though.

The weather and climate encompass
The stars and other terrestrials
All of them celebrate the midnight dew that passes
For it gives them a chilling effect that lasts.

You are just temporary as I know
But the memoirs you give are somehow longing too
The scents of midnight dew
Is something everlasting that takes a blow.

ON THE WINGS OF LOVE

No matter how distant you are
I will fly to your place at far
My wings will spread out
And start to soar high with no doubt.

This is the only remedy I know
That our love would pursue
Getting near to you my love
Riding my wings above.

The limited power I have my dear
It will be utilized to get you near
Believing earnestly the love so real
I am brave enough with no deal.

The grasp of my tiny hands
To a little hope, I bear to stand
Emphasizing the great emotion
The pure and honest motivation.

On my wide spirited wings
Here I am now flying
To the space of delectation
Wait for me my great inspiration.

On my way, I might encounter
The turbulence of sagging air
I am not afraid to go on
Holding my faith in my destination.

TEENAGE LOVE

I had once a teenage love, lack of expression
I was afraid and ashamed to display my feelings on
We were lovers but I just kept my emotions
I pretended to him that I had no attraction.

Deep inside, I was sunk in my pretention
His eagerness was gone, he was tired alone
For he thought to him, I had no love as I've shown.
Slowly I felt too much pain as he neglected me

He really believed I was not falling for him deeply
For I am a great pretender hiding my feelings
intensively
Though my heart was longing for him immensely.
My teenage love gave me more lessons

To love again with the utmost reasons
My teenage love was gone I mourned
I cried out loud my tears told him about my late
reactions.
By not showing my heartfelt emotion.

PROMISED LOVE

He offered her an infinity ring
Promising her to be a queen
That in his life no other women
And he would give her, his name.

The most dream scenario of every woman
Seeing her most beloved man
Kneeling in front of her no adamance
But heartily asking for her lifetime romance.

An expression of man's humility
Uttering words of promissory
That until to the most eternity
They will love each other truly.

A woman is convinced and amazed
That she gave her biggest yes
Both of them were engaged
Sooner they would be wed.

Their eyes met across in parallel
Their dreams are about to reach and deal
Their love brings a nest to unveil
They are building a family to reveal.

MIXED FEELINGS

The heart keeps all our inner feelings
Maybe gladiolus or sorrows interconnecting
The mind dictates the consciousness of our physical
being
They go synchronizing for us to have a mindful living.

No one would go beyond over the other
They are in equilibrium as they go together
The dictate of the mind collaborates with the beating
of the heart
As they go partaking the function as body parts.

Mind is the intangible thought of a soul
The heart can touch the humanity at all
There's no reason for them to go against in thrall
But they should go parallel in one direction sole.

Loving someone requires your heart and mind
Never let the heart dominates and forgets the mind
You might go wrong if you put one behind
Weigh it in an isostatic measure to find.

In this world of many strifes and temptations
We should think twice before taking actions
Empathic heart and mindful in our direction
Nurturing both as we live with aspiration.

I BELIEVE

I believe I can do it all
The heightening triumphant soul
I can fly beneath my shining tool
Bringing up the high-spirited rule

How difficult the task is
I can succeed as I practice
My strong determination sees
That I am able to do this.

Nothing is impossible my dear friend
If we are empowered to apprehend
That I strongly believe I can attain
Beholding all that pertains.

I can reach my goal as I go on
Believing firmly in my own
For the one, up above his throne
Guiding me as I perform.

Wherever I may be brought
Of my tomorrow's moving foot
I believe I can fulfill my thought
Yes, I do for my belief is for the truth.

AMAZING LOVE

Love hurts when loving failed
It seems pain couldn't be healed
But one day you would be amazed
You fall in love again, as you once wished.

The stars are aligned, sparkling in your eyes
They are the ingredients or the best spices
Their aromatic sense coordinates with a prize
The sweetness penetrates to the bones of different
sizes.

Love Oh love thank you for a feeling of upliftment
Happiness overload as of this very moment
I forget all the failures that once happened
As if I am floating on a cloud nine.

No whisper of harmful despair
Nor no beat of little fear
I am now in complete surrender
To the best feeling, I felt ever.

This is in the name of love that I survive
Discarding all the negativities I hide
Living a hopeful life to revive
To you my love I ponder my whole life.

MORE THAN JUST A TREASURE

Moments with loved ones are my most treasure
That gave my life a complete pleasure
Forming my pieces as a whole caricature
Reminiscing golden moments in nature.

Nothing compares to the love we share
To someone, we loved forever
Each second, minute and hour, or even year
Marked in my inner being so tender.

The best feeling that I could remember
It genuinely has something to ponder
That leaves remarkable dates ever
Golden moments as I could utter.

Bonding with the family and loved ones
That when kids grow bigger they could tell to
everyone
Their most golden moments with us at once
Would be the footprints that they would bring beyond.

The good camaraderie of the family
Of everyone that we share daily
Would be the augmented love every day
That we must love to treasure as one truly.

THE YEAR 2020

This has been a very crucial year
When I lost my dearest mother
Returning from home two weeks after
Covid-19 brought us fear.

A very unique season for all
A world halted seemed its downfall
No one is exempted rich or poor
We all closed our doors.

The government stood firm to protect
The shivering crowd of people to seek
The utmost help for food to take
Unity came in knocking to partake.

The silence at night didn't mean its peace
But of fearful life that brought no ease
Everyone pleaded to God to cease
The scary virus that invades our happiness.

Twenty-twenty you are the most remarkable year
That everyone on Earth has to remember
But despite the hazardous event, you brought us here
Still, we are very grateful to God our Father.

For sparing us from that pandemic fever
He continuously covers us with his divine hands ever
Letting us live adequately and healthier
This gives us more lessons to learn.

Valuing what we have and one another
And to beseech God saying our prayers
Treasuring all our family members
That life is the most sacred here on Earth.

Now 2020 is about to say us adieu
Let us together see the nearest view
Of 2021 coming to us anew
May this new year delete the bad experiences we
drew.

Nothing we have to fight the challenges
Only our strong faith in God that changes
The heavy predicament we all experience
We altogether repent and draw near to God asking for
His forgiveness.

WHAT IF?

The sun rises in the west
Showing its sunlight at its best
Monastery grooving from the east
My love fades at its weakest.

Please mind not going against my wishes
Instead, collaborate on my ideas at the highest
Subsidence occurs not to aggravate its mess
Though they are not meant to resist.

Love me tenderly as I do
Show me clearly the essence of you
Never mind what others may go through
But sincerely trying to

Oh, believe me not to do so.
What if...it's my last day
When do you show me
A love that so honestly

Just tell me sincerely.
My heart aches upon knowing
That someone I trust truly is ignoring
My selfless love is now annoying
Before I go let me know not so hurting.

GOD BE WITH YOU

Be strong my friend
Keep strengthened
Fight for your right Neng
Life must go on whatever happened

You are so beautiful
Your life is meaningful
Some trials are given not a downfall
But to become more reliable.

Keep your head high
No one can compare your good sight
You have a clean heart at height
The ailment could be cured not for freight.

Stay positive with good thoughts
Link to better people
Who can enlighten your bad mood
Look forward to a better cure.

Many have shared their stories
Of life swing as your memories
They are the living epitome of a heroine
You are young and gorgeous so maintain.

Live your useful life through
Keep forwarding don't stop to
You have a lot to thank to
For God loves you.

If there are tests of faith
Don't be disturbed but have set
A goal to take not to upset
You have a way to go don't reset.

Fight for your right
God had put a light
For you to delight
Be well and hold Him tight.

NATURE'S WAY

Long to see the beautiful flowers
In the lovely garden of sunflowers
Love to breathe the fresh air
When no one could ever fear.

The sweet birds singing in the trees
Nowhere to hear nowadays
The children laughing in the loudest
No one could hear them the simplest.

Nature's touch slowly separates
Humanity is tattered indebts
No one is brave to explore out dates
What they have is to aim for the safest.

People and nature have their space
In this era of pandemic disease
Everyone is afraid to expose to places
They want to stay at home as based.

Far from the nature's touch simplifying the mass
Address the issue as the horrible grass
Non-sense to express the best trust

When no one could ever grasp.
After all, we must be in the middle class
Sensing the seasons of no clash
Counting the messages we must
To feel nature's touch at last.

REWRITE THE STAR

As a very prominent terrestrial body
Respect and honor are sent to you today
This is the most effective way
To make the best message as can be.

Rewrite the stars to let you know
The most descent feeling to show
That in fact, somehow it will grow
The transcending brightness will glow.

The stars of a momentary prescription
That leads to the wholesome aspiration
Is privileged to be heard and read in dominion
For the righteous and admirable supplication.

The best visualization that predicts
The direction that percepts
That encompasses and evicts
The neutralization that nearly accepts.

Tell the enormous purpose of unity
Wave high the aspect of spirituality
Salute the honorable against the mortality
Rewrite oh! rewrite what is written mistakenly.

Match the matchless infinity
Block the issues going on miserably
For sometimes it amends the misery
Hold on to oblivion of any mystery.

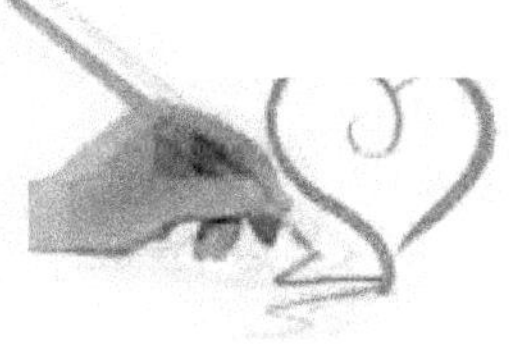

The justifying fears unload their clarity
It paves more to the places of sanctity
Creating lifeful star mission of divinity
Spilling out at the congested area of majesty.

Crop and edit the unfitted acts
Uproot the grasses that surround the tract
Slow down to the rough road of the truck
Say hi to the starlet who is the prince luck.

God has created the moon and the stars
On his hands, all of them were made near or far
The stars' effect of creation so popular
Connecting the universal spectacular.

Redeem the humanity in salient mark
Relocate the permanent position of the dark
Shine Oh! stars in the farthest part
So I rewrite the meaning mistakenly written at that.

Renew the contract of the stars to start
Replenish the corrupted light before it departs
Regain the energy that it has about to part
Make sure you remake all the crafted arts.

Due to the unsettled chaotic gap
No one can adjoin and tap
But instead, bridge the missing lap
Foresee the enlightenment of the Lord God.

Thy star bears the basic light
So we pursue the glimmering brightly.

ABOUT THE AUTHOR

GIRLIE E. CATANUS graduated Bachelor in Elementary Education Major in Reading at West Visayas State University, Lapaz Iloilo City.

She also graduated Master of Arts in Education majoring in Language Education at New Era University, Quezon City, and is currently enrolled in Doctor of Philosophy Program at Pacific Intercontinental College, Las Pinas City.

Girlie is already 20 years in the service as a public school teacher. She is also Division Trainer and Writer.

9 786214 702596